© Snap Productions Ltd

8 Reservoir Road, Birkenhead, CH42 8LJ

Printed 2010

Designed by Bag of Badgers

ISBN 978-0-9566075-1-5

1 3 5 7 9 10 8 6 4 2

Printed in China

FAMILY RECORD BOOK

Parents

Mother:

Date of Birth:

Father:

Date of Birth:

Children

Our family tree

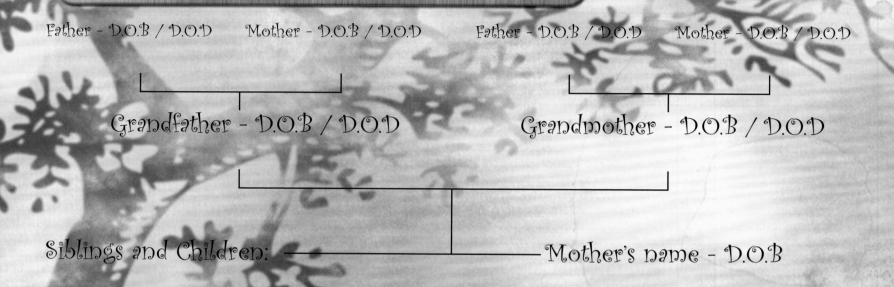

Father - D.O.B / D.O.D   Mother - D.O.B / D.O.D   Father - D.O.B / D.O.D   Mother - D.O.B / D.O.D

Grandfather - D.O.B / D.O.D   Grandmother - D.O.B / D.O.D

Siblings and Children: Mother's name - D.O.B

Children and Partners - D.O.B

Grandchildren - D.O.B.

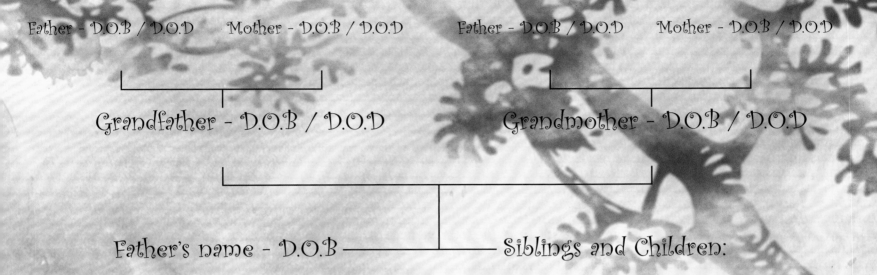

Father - D.O.B / D.O.D   Mother - D.O.B / D.O.D   Father - D.O.B / D.O.D   Mother - D.O.B / D.O.D

Grandfather - D.O.B / D.O.D   Grandmother - D.O.B / D.O.D

Father's name - D.O.B   Siblings and Children:

Mum and Dad

Mum's name:

What we call her:

Where she was born:

Where she grew up:

Mum's first memory:

What Mum was like as a teenager:

Mum's job:

Dad's name:

What we call him:

Where he was born:

Where he grew up:

Dad's first memory:

What Dad was like as a teenager:

Dad's job:

How Mum and Dad met:

Where they got married:

How old they were when they first became parents:

What Mum liked about Dad:

What Dad liked about Mum:

Their ages when they got married:

A picture of Mum and Dad

11

Our Grandparents

What we call our Mum's Mother:

Where she was born:

Where she grew up:

What job she did:

How old she was when she
got married:

What we call our Mum's Father:

Where he was born:

Where he grew up:

What job he did:

How old he was when he
got married:

A picture of our Mum's parents

What we call our Dad's Mother:

Where she was born:

Where she grew up:

What job she did:

How old she was when she
got married:

What we call our Dad's Father:

Where he was born:

Where he grew up:

What job he did:

How old he was when he
got married:

A picture of our Dad's parents

Family pets

Our pet's name:

The type of animal our pet is:

Who does our pet belong to:

Our pet's favourite food:

Our pet's worst habit:

How our pet makes us laugh:

The person who looks after our pet the most:

Why we love our pet:

Our pet's name:

The type of animal our pet is:

Who does our pet belong to:

Our pet's favourite food:

Our pet's worst habit:

How our pet makes us laugh:

The person who looks after our pet the most:

Why we love our pet:

Our pet's name:

The type of animal our pet is:

Who does our pet belong to:

Our pet's favourite food:

Our pet's worst habit:

How our pet makes us laugh:

The person who looks after our pet the most:

Why we love our pet:

A picture of our pet

A picture of our pet

15

Special family members

Our special relative:

Where they live:

How often we see them:

What we like about them:

Special days we've spent together:

Our favourite memory of them:

A picture of us with

A picture of us with

Our special relative:

Where they live:

How often we see them:

What we like about them:

Special days we've spent together:

Our favourite memory of them:

Our special relative:

Where they live:

How often we see them:

What we like about them:

Special days we've spent together:

Our favourite memory of them:

17

Family celebrations

Here is a record of some special events we shared as a family.

The special celebration:

Date of event:

Where we held the event:

Who attended the event:

Where we stayed before and after the event:

What we ate:

Special clothes we wore:

Funny things that happened:

What we remember most about the event:

A picture of us with

The special celebration:

Date of event:

Where we held the event:

Who attended the event:

The special celebration:

Date of event:

Where we held the event:

Who attended the event:

A picture of us with

A picture of us with

19

Where we live

Our address is:

The type of property we live in is:

Who has the best bedroom:

What we like about our house:

What we would change if we could:

What chores the children have:

Who cleans the house:

Who does the gardening:

Our nearest park:

Our next door neighbours are called:

How we get on with them:

Other people we know in our street:

What we don't like about living here:

The place we live is:

How long it takes to get to school:

What we like about living here:

Where we would like to live if we could choose:

A picture of our house

Mealtimes

Who cooks the most:

Who does the washing up:

The best meal Mum cooks:

The best meal Dad cooks:

What we like cooking together:

Where we eat our evening meal:

Who we eat it with:

How often we eat together as a family:

Best TV dinner:

Our favourite pudding:

22

The worst family meal we ever had:

Why it was so bad:

The best family meal we ever had:

Why it was so good:

Our family eating together

Family friends

Mum's friends she's known all her life:

How they met:

Mum's favourite memories of their friendship:

How often we see them:

What we enjoy doing together:

Dad's friends he's known all his life:

How they met:

Dad's favourite memories of their friendship:

How often we see them:

What we enjoy doing together:

Other family friends:

Where they live: | How often we see them: | What we enjoy doing together:

School days

Where Mum went to school:

Her favourite subject was:

Her worst subject was:

The naughtiest thing she did at school was:

How old she was when she left school:

Her best memory of her school days:

Where Dad went to school:

His favourite subject was:

His worst subject was:

The naughtiest thing he did at school was:

How old he was when he left school:

His best memory of his school days:

School photo

Where the children in our family
go to school:
Name:
school:
School uniform:

Name:
school:
School uniform:

Name:
school:
School uniform:

Name:
school:
School uniform:

The member of our family who
works hardest at school:

The member of our family who gets
into most trouble:

Who likes school:

Who doesn't like school:

School trips we've been on:

Days out together

Here are some of the special days out that we have shared together:

Where we went on our day out:

The date:

Who came along on our day out:

How we travelled there:

What made us laugh:

Some of the things we did and saw on our day out:

Us on a trip together to

Best thing about the day:

28

Where we went on our day out:

The date:

Who came along on our day out:

How we travelled there:

What made us laugh:

Some of the things we did and saw on our day out:

Best thing about the day:

Where we went on our day out:

The date:

Who came along on our day out:

How we travelled there:

What made us laugh:

Some of the things we did and saw on our day out:

Best thing about the day:

Us on a trip together to

Family holidays

The type of holidays Mum had as a child:

The first holiday they took as a couple:

The type of holidays Dad had as a child:

The first holiday they took as parents: What they remember about it:

Mum's favourite childhood holiday memory:

Dad's favourite childhood holiday memory:

Our family on holiday at....

What we enjoy doing on holiday:

What we argue about on holiday:

Our family on holiday at....

Our favourite family holiday and why:

Our worst family holiday and why:

Places we want to visit in the future:

Our family on holiday at....

Our family Christmas

Where we usually celebrate Christmas:

Who usually visits us at Christmas:

How we usually celebrate Christmas:

The most unusual present one of us
has received:

Other people who have spent
Christmas with us in the past:

Christmas in

Unusual places we have
celebrated Christmas:

Our best ever Christmas and why:

The funniest Christmas story
in our family:

Our worst ever Christmas and why:

Christmas in

Memorable events

Here are some of the events that we have experienced with the support of our family. They may be performances we've taken part in, ceremonies we've attended, sad family events, or events related to hobbies or interests we share as a family:

Memorable event:

Date:

Who was present:

What happened:

Special memories about the event:

Picture of memorable event:

Memorable event:

Date:

Who was present:

What happened:

Special memories about the event:

Picture of memorable event:

Memorable event:

Date:

Who was present:

What happened:

Special memories about the event:

Looking back

The achievement of which
Mum is most proud:

Things Mum would do differently:

Things Dad would do differently:

The achievement of which
Dad is most proud:

How Mum and Dad felt
becoming parents:

Mum's biggest regret:

Dad's biggest regret:

How being parents changed
their lives:

Advice that Mum and Dad give about growing up:

Fears we have about the future:

Advice that Mum and Dad give about work:

What Mum and Dad think we'll be when we grow up:

What we want to be when we grow up:

What Mum and Dad's greatest wishes are for us for the future: